MW00366000

mom, you're one of a kind

by max & lucy®

6th™
avenue
books

AOL Time Warner Book Group
An AOL Time Warner Company

6th Avenue Books is an imprint of AOL Time Warner Book Group
An AOL Time Warner Book Group
1271 Avenue of the Americas
New York, N.Y. 10020

6th™
avenue
books

10 9 8 7 6 5 4 3 2 1

ISBN:1-931722-32-3

Manufactured in China

mothers are forever

She knows us like no one else. Her hugs melt away the hurts of every day life. We call her Mom, and she is truly a treasured gift. Once we move away from home, we sometimes forget all that she has done and sacrificed to make our lives better. As the years pass by, however, we come to appreciate her more and more. This book is our testament to all that Mom's do every day.

If you're reading this, you're either about to share this book with your Mom (or Mom-type person) or you received it from someone who wants you to know just how special you are.

The fact that either of those possibilities has happened is something to celebrate. Which is exactly what this little book is about. Thanks Mom, there is truly no one like you.

max & lucy

a few motherly thoughts of your own

mom, you're
one of a kind...

...because...

you let me stay up late

we're two of a kind

you love me, baggage and all

i look up to you

you always find the right words

you know when i'm feeling blue

you indulge me

you taught me to be myself,
with no strings attached

i came along
and you made some changes

somehow you know
when i need you

you are a very stylish girl

i'd be lost without you

you pushed me to new heights

your arms are always open

We go well together

you help me when i fumble

Without you
i'd be a fish out of water

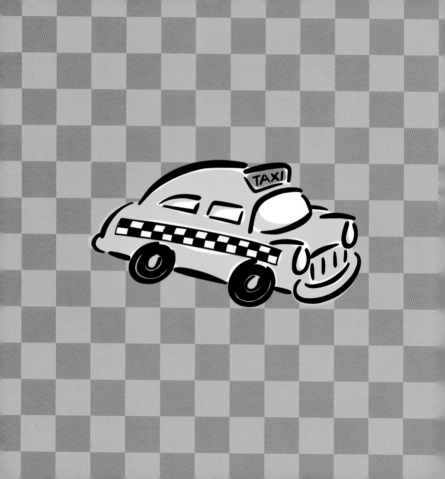

you never turned the meter on

you never forget to love me

you get better as i get older

you let me keep the strays

you smooth out my rough spots

you always take my calls

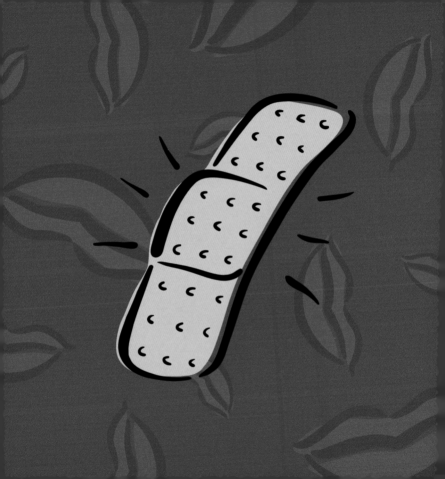

you fix my hurts

you're magical

your love is unconditional

you made me eat my Vegetables

you make me feel like a winner

you make me laugh

you allowed me to stretch

i can relax when i'm with you

you did my laundry

you turn a house into a home

you're the queen

you're one of a kind

acknowledgments

Yes, Mom, we thank you for this book. After all, we know you'd call if we didn't mention you here. In addition to our appreciation of your contributions to our lives, we offer more specific thanks to Bradley Smith and Aaron Thompson for creating artwork that so delightfully conveys our emotions and sentiments. And, of course, to our friends at 6th Avenue Books, we send our deepest appreciation for making our Mothers proud – a book in their honor.

max & lucy

about max & lucy

Max & Lucy is a tiny little company in Phoenix, Arizona, that makes greeting cards, notes and other fun ways for people to correspond. Founded by Russ Haan and named after two cats who live in a warehouse, the company is now owned by Russ and two good friends, Mike Oleskow and Bradley Smith. As the author in the crowd, Russ penned most of this book, but humbly admits that without his partners, the words would not have been the same. To learn more about Max & Lucy, feel free to visit the company's web site at www.maxandlucy.com.

max & lucy®